101 Curious Questions…

Ice Breaker, game, or just to dig deeper into one's psyche

By Celeste Camille Jones

Dedicated to my auntie Camille who had a curious mind and a zest for living life to the fullest.

IF....

1. IF you could be a collector of any one item what would it be?

2. IF you could have any animal in the World as a pet, what kind of animal would you have? IF this animal could do any trick of your choice what trick would it be?

3. IF you had to rename yourself, what first name would you choose? Middle name?

4. IF you could be born into any family in the World with all the benefits as well as the shortcomings and even scandals associated with that family name, which family would you choose to be part of?

5. IF you had to pick 2 musical artists to listen to for the rest of your life, including past, present, future, and collaborations.... And could not listen to any other musicians, whom would you choose?

6. IF you could be a contestant on any one reality show that is currently on, which show would you choose and why? Which one would you want to host?

7. IF you could 'jump' to any location on Earth but someone would die who is 7 degrees of separation from you every time you did, would you? How about if the person was just 2 degrees of separation from you?

8. IF you had to be born again but had to choose your nationality, race, and gender

...different from your current identity, what would you choose?

9. IF you had to say...
'WHO or WHAT were
you in your past life?'
HOW did you die?

10. IF you had to choose one to keep, would you pick your arms or legs? Your eyes or ears?

11. IF you could change your birth order with your siblings, would you? .... IF you are an only child would you choose to have siblings?

12. IF you could be someone's muse... would it be an artist, musician, or writer? WHY?

13. IF you had to pick one color as a 'favorite' which color do you choose? What color do you get the most compliments when wearing? What color describes your personality?

14. IF you had a choice, what is the first thing you'd want someone to notice about you? What do people normally compliment you on?

15. IF $20,000 were put into your bank account right now WOULD you use the money to move, change occupations, pay debt, do something or go somewhere fun, or buy something you have been wanting?

16. IF you had the opportunity to give anyone you know a truth pill, WHO would you give it to? WHAT would you want to know?

17. IF somehow you knew for sure someone you cared for deeply would be convicted of a crime and sentenced to 10 years in prison... would you help them hide/flee and risk becoming an accessory to the crime OR would you turn them in? What if there were a $100,000 reward?

18. IF you had to write a song about a recent happening in your life, what would the title of the song be?

19. IF you could go back in time and be a part of any historical event, which would you choose and why?

20. IF you wrote an autobiography, what would the title be?

21. The president wanted to build a wall... IF you could build a wall around anything what/ where would it be? Would it keep people/ animals out or would it keep them in?

22. IF you had 48 hours to live, where would you go within physical constraints of travel and time/ schedules etc....?

23. IF you had to teach a class right now on any one thing that you've mastered, what would the class be called?

24. IF you could change one thing about yourself what would it be? About your partner?

25. IF you had to re-experience a single day in your past, what day or experience would you choose?

26. IF someone narrated your life, WHO would it be?

27. Lays had a potato chip flavor contest... IF they did this again, what flavor would you submit?

28. IF you could turn any activity into an Olympic sport, what activity do you think you'd have a good chance of winning a medal for?

29. IF you could make a 30 second phone call to yourself at any point in your life, past or future, what time/age period would you call and what would you say?

30. IF you could choose your dreams when you sleep, what do you prefer to dream about?

31. IF you were to open your refrigerator right now, WHAT would you find? What is one food item you cannot live without?

WHAT....

32. WHAT is a mistake you had to make more than once to learn the lesson it was teaching?

33. WHAT is the most recent act of generosity you have done for someone? WHAT is the most generous thing someone has ever done for you?

34. You have 24 hours to live! WHAT do you want to eat (no budget)?

35. WHAT do you wish you were better at?

36. WHAT is the last thing you GOOGLED? (check your search history if you forgot)

37. WHAT is the biggest financial mistake you have made?

38. WHAT is the ideal age to retire? How much do you need in the bank to retire comfortably? What do you want to do when you retire?

39. WHAT superpower would you choose to have just for today?

40. WHAT is your favorite trait in yourself? Your worst? What traits do you admire in others?

41. WHAT would a sitcom about your life be called?

42. WHAT are 3 other career paths you've considered other than the one you're in? Has anyone ever suggested you missed your calling in a career?

43. WHAT is the most expensive food item you have ever ordered on a menu or bought?

44. WHAT is the most expensive possession you own other than your car or home?

45. WHAT is your choice 'outlet' when under stress?

46. WHAT book are
you reading right
now? WHAT book that
you've read before
would
you recommend
highly?

47. WHAT'S a large purchase you made that you could look back and say "that was money well spent!" (not car or house)? How about a regrettable purchase?

48. WHAT is something you are confident that no one else you know has done?

49. An investor has $1 million to invest into your new business... WHAT business will you be opening/ starting?

50. WHAT book or movie has had the greatest impact on the way you think about life?

51. WHAT are the 3 most used apps on your cell phone? 3 websites you make the most purchases from?

52. WHAT would you say is the 'best' use of time you ever spent on yourself?

53. WHAT 'weird' food combination do you enjoy?

54. WHAT is the best way to start the day?

55. WHAT is the most recent food you discovered you like or rediscovered?

56. WHAT career would you be great at? Bad at? What job do you think you were born to do?

57. WHAT'S the most annoying question people ask you regularly?

58. WHAT'S something you believe everyone should do at least once in their lives?

59. WHAT'S the hardest lesson you learned? The most expensive lesson?

60. WHAT do you like most about your immediate family?

61. WHAT'S the most immature or childish thing you still do?

62. WHAT chapters would you separate your autobiography into?

63. WHAT stats from your life would you most like to see?

64. WHAT would you change your name to if you were the opposite gender?

65. WHAT is your go-to snack? If you had to eat the same 3 meals every single day, what would they be?

66. WHAT are all the jobs you've ever had?

Which did you like the most? The worst?

67. WHAT is the last major goal you accomplished? What is the next goal you are actively working to accomplish now?

68. WHAT is the most ridiculous rule you currently must follow?

69. WHAT'S invisible to the eye but you wish you could see?

70. WHAT tells you the most about a person?

71. WHAT are 5 places you really want to visit before you die?

72. WHAT odd quirks did you pick up from your parents? Does your body have any odd quirks?

73. WHAT movie never gets old no matter how many times you've seen it?

74. WHAT are you kind of snobby about?

75. WHICH living celebrity would make the best President of the United States?

76. On Valentine's Day you have 3 gifts… a diamond necklace, roses, and your time. WHICH would you give to your significant other, your friend, your mom?

77. WHICH decision in your life would you take back if you could and make a different decision?

WOULD you rather...

78. WOULD you rather be good looking, rich, healthy, OR happy?

79. WOULD you rather give your phone number to a cutie in a hooptie or an unattractive person in a Bentley?

80. WOULD you or have you dated someone younger than you? What are the advantages and disadvantages? What is the youngest age you would date? How about older (same questions)?

81. WOULD you rather be the trophy wife/husband OR the breadwinner? WHAT would be the ideal profession for your spouse?

82. WOULD you rather live in a remote, peaceful village and only know about major events that affect you only in a life-or-death manner OR live in the epicentre of a big city and know every little piece of news as it happens?

83. WOULD you stay
with your significant
other if they found out
they were the parent
of a child they were
unaware of?

84. WOULD you rather your death be a tragedy blasted all over the news Worldwide OR a peaceful death only to be known by your friends and family?

WHEN AND WHY...

85. WHEN you first meet someone, do you care more about looks, personality, or finances? WHICH 1 of the 3 would you say you yourself bring to the table?

86. WHEN you meet someone new, potential friend or lover, do you tend to want to know what your family and friends think of them before settling on your final opinion of them? Do you care what others think? WHY?

NAME WHO...

87. NAME as many friends as you can that you've known for more than 15yrs? 10yrs? 5yrs? WHO are your most recent acquaintances?

88. People come into your life for one of three reasons: a lifetime, a reason, or a season. NAME one person you've known for each category.

89. WHO is your celebrity look-alike? Celebrity crush? Your celebrity BFF (in your mind)?

DO YOU or HAVE YOU...

90. DO you tend to be more religious or spiritual? WHAT is the difference to you?

91. DO you gravitate more towards being alone or conversing with others? Do you prefer to be around others who are introverted or extroverted?

92. DID you or WOULD you go to your 10yr/ 20yr/ 30yr high school reunion? Why or Why Not? Do you keep in touch with anyone from high school?

93. Typically, DO you look within for answers or to others?

94. In your lifetime HAVE you dealt with more givers or takers? What do you consider yourself?

95. HAVE you ever had to put a restraining or no trespass order on someone? Have you ever wanted to?

96. DO you have a personal philosophy by which you live?

97. HAVE you ever had
an event in your life
that defied
explanation?

98. HAVE you dated
outside of your race?
How do you feel about
mixed-race couples?

MISCELLANEOUS...

99. Empty life and meaningful death OR meaningful life and empty death?

100. IS there anything you have struggled with your entire life?

101. You just won a new super yacht; you must name your boat in the next 60 seconds, or you lose it! GO!

BONUS….

Were you inspired by this book to come up with your own questions? Below is space for you to add them:

102.

103.

104.

105.

106.

107.

108.

109.

110.

"There is never an end to the questions within a curious mind."

-Celeste Camille Jones